South Pole Santa

Written and illustrated by
Janice Hostetter

BUMBLEBEE
BOOKSHELF

For my Wild Boys
who sit with the mall Santa
so the littles will.

And for Brady
Because of that
one time.

DEAR

SANTA CLAUS

SANTA 'S WORKSHOP

NORTH POLE

Sophie loves ice skating,

making cookies
with Mommy,

and decorating with Daddy.

"I love presents the **most**," Sam says.

"Christmas isn't about **presents**," Mommy explains. **Christmas** is about **family** and the **animals** that you **love**."

Sam writes his letter to **santa.**

He wants a ***RACECAR***, a chocolate bar, and a pet **FISH.**

Sophie writes her letter.

Dear Santa,
I want a microphone so I can sing and dance. And some roller skates if you have room.

Sophie delivers **yummy** cookies to her friends.

"Want some **hot cocoa,** Sam?"

"No thanks,"
says Sam.

"I'm helping everyone mail their letters. It takes a long time for mail to get from the **south pole** to the **North pole**."

Sophie sings
Christmas carols
with her friends.

Finally, Christmas Eve comes.

The animals decorate the **biggest** tree in Antarctica.

It is **beautiful**.

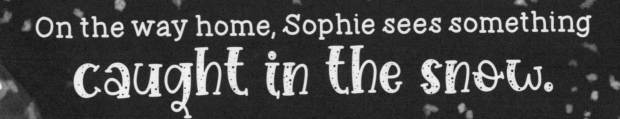

On the way home, Sophie sees something
caught in the snow.

"What is it?"
Amelia asks.

"It looks like a
sleigh," Jia says.

Sophie digs and digs.

Amelia and Jia help.

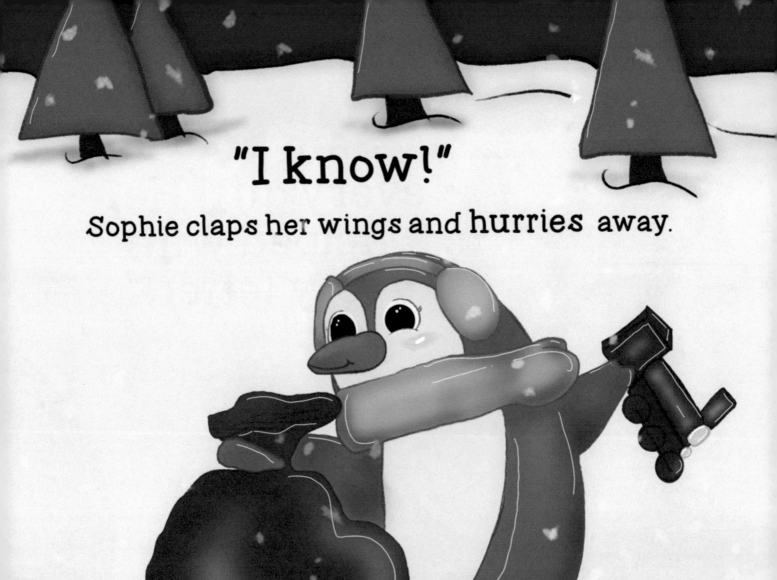

"I know!"

Sophie claps her wings and hurries away.

Together, the animals deliver every gift before the sun comes up.

"This is the best Christmas Eve **EVER,"**

says Sophie.

"It has been fun," Sam agrees.

"You are our very own South Pole Santa, Sam!"

Sam laughs.

Christmas
morning
comes
and
all
the
animals
rush
to
the
tree.

Sam looks around at his friends. He feels happy to see them happy.

"Don't you like your presents, Sam?" Mama asks.

"I do like the presents," Sam smiles, "But the best part of Christmas is being with the animals I love."

about the
Author

Janice Hostetter is a debut author of beautifully illustrated picture books, fulfilling a lifelong dream that began with scribbling stories in spiral notebooks. Her upbringing in Appalachia has infused her tales with the warm wonder of her home region, drawing from the rich storytelling traditions of her childhood. As a proud mother to five human babies and two fur babies, she finds endless inspiration in the laughter and chaos of family life.

When Janice isn't penning tales or immersed in a good book, you can find her behind the lens, capturing the beauty of nature through photography. She finds joy sharing cherished moments with her loved ones and connecting with the great outdoors during camping trips. Through her creative pursuits and love for exploration, she continues to weave tales that spark the imaginations of young readers.

"Another cute little story with a big message!"

★★★★★

-Debbie
- Head Christmas Candy chef
- mother of author
- #1 Mimi

Don't let this be my only review!
Head over to Amazon and let me know what you love
about Sam & Sophie!

www.amazon.com/authors/bumblebeebookshelf

Let's keep in touch!
For news about upcoming adventures, follow @jhostetterbooks on Instagram
Send fan art to jhostetterbooks@gmail.com and I'll show it on my page!

Check Out Our other Titles:

The Ballad of Levi Locust

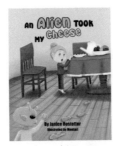

An Alien Took my Cheese

Grandma Gets an Upgrade

Moose and Frog Go for a Walk

BUMBLEBEE
B O O K S H E L F